THE POWER OF THANKSGIVING

"In everything give thanks: for this is the will of God in Christ Jesus concerning you."

1theo5:18

By
Franklin N. Abazie

The Power of Thanksgiving

COPYRIGHT 2018 BY Franklin N Abazie
ISBN: 978:1-945-133-6-33
All right reserved. This book or any portion thereof may not be reproduced or used in any manner whatsoever without the express written permission of the publisher, except for the use of brief quotations in a book review. All Bible quotes are from King James Version and others as noted.

Published by: F N ABAZIE PUBLISHING HOUSE---
a.k.a,
Empowerment Bookstore:

That I may publish with the voice of thanksgiving and tell of all thy wondrous works. **Psalms26:7**

To order additional copies, wholesales or booking: Call the Church office (973-372-7518)
or Empowerment Bookstore Hotline 973-393-8518
Worship address:
343 Sanford Avenue Newark New Jersey 07106
Administrative Head Office address:
33 Schley Street Newark New Jersey 07112
Email:pastorfranknto@yahoo.com
Website www.fnabaziehealingministries.org
Publishing House: www.fnabaziepublishinghouse.org

This book is a production of F N Abazie Publishing House.

A publication Arms of Miracle of God Ministries 2018
First Edition

CONTENTS

THE MANDATE OF THE COMMISSION...........iv

ARMS OF THE COMMISSION............................v

INTRODUCTION...viii

CHAPTER 1

1. What is Thanksgiving? 39

CHAPTER 2

2. How to Give Quality Thanks to God..................47

CHAPTER 3

3. Prayer of Salvation...68

CHAPTER 4

4. About the Author..77

THE MANDATE OF THE COMMISSION

"THE MOMENT IS DUE TO IMPACT YOUR WORLD THROUGH THE REVIVAL OF THE HEALING & MIRACLE MINISTRY OF JESUS CHRIST OF NAZARETH.

I AM SENDING YOU TO RESTORE HEALTH UNTO THEE AND I WILL HEAL THEE OF THY WOUNDS, SAID THE LORD OF HOST."

ARMS OF THE COMMISSION

1) F N Abazie Ministries-Miracle of God Ministries (Miracle Chapel Intl)

2) F N Abazie TV Ministries: Global Television Ministry Outreach.

3) F N Abazie Radio Ministries: Radio Broadcasting Outreach.

4) F N Abazie Publishing House: Book Publication.

5) F N Abazie Bible School: also called Word of Healing Bible School (W.O.H.B.S)

6) F N Abazie Evangelistic Ass: Miracle of God Ministries: Global Crusade

7) Empowerment Bookstore: Book distribution.

8) F N Abazie Helping Hands: Meeting the help of the needy world wide

9) F N Abazie Disaster Recovery Mission: Global Disaster Recovery.

10) F N Abazie Prison Ministry: Prison Ministry for all convicts "Second chance"

Some of our ministry arms are waiting the appointed time to commence

FAVOR CONFESSION

Father thank you for making me righteous and accepted through the blood of Jesus Christ. Because of that, I am blessed and highly favored by God. I am the subject of your affection. Your favor surrounds me as a shield, and the first thing that people see around me is your favored shield.

Thank you that I have favor with you and man today. All day long people go out of their way to bless me and help me. I have favor with everyone that I deal with today. Doors that were once closed are now opened for me. I receive preferential treatment, and I have special privileges, I am Gods favored child.

No good thing will he withhold from me. Because of Gods favor my enemies cannot triumph over my life. I have supernatural increase and promotion. I declare restoration to everything that the devil has stolen from my life. I have honor in the midst of my adversaries and an increase in assets, especially in real estate and expansion of territories.

Because I am highly favored by God, I experience great victories, supernatural turnarounds, and miraculous breakthrough in the midst of great impossibilities. I receive recognition, prominence, and honor. Petitions are granted to me even by ungodly authorities. Policies, rules, regulations, and laws are changed and reverse on my behalf.

I win battles that I don't even have to fight, because God fights them for me. This is the day, the set time and the designated moment for me to experience the free favor of God, that profusely and lavishly abound on my behalf in Jesus name. Amen.

INTRODUCTION

"In everything give thanks: for this is the will of God in Christ Jesus concerning you."
1theo5:18

Every year millions of Americans make plans ahead of time to celebrate thanksgiving holiday. Well, do not just celebrate thanksgiving as a holiday, have a genuine reason to thank the Lord for His hand upon your life.

In this book, I have explained what it means to give quality thanks to God. One of the greatest mystery of the kingdom of God is the mystery of thanksgiving. Outside the Kingdom of God, most people will only give thanks when someone does anything good for them. In the Kingdom of God we give thanks ahead of time.

In thanksgiving we appreciate God as the source and doer of everything that happened in our life.

This book encourage everyone to practice the act thanksgiving as a lifestyle. Thanksgiving is an attitude of gratitude. I once heard that misery loves company. No miserable man or woman can attract the glory of God.

I guarantee you, if you give thanks well, you will never be stranded in life. We must make thanksgiving a lifestyle. Until you learn to give thanks well, you are not ready to prosper in the kingdom of God. Thanksgiving have power, what kind of power one may ask? Thanksgiving have power to set anyone up for the next miracle.

One leper who returned to Jesus to say "thank you Lord" He was made perfectly whole. *"And he said unto him, Arise, go thy way: thy faith hath made thee whole."* **Luke17:19.**

It is my prayer that you embrace thanksgiving as a lifestyle, you will never regret it in life.

Happy Reading!

HIS DESTINY WAS THE CROSS….

HIS PURPOSE WAS LOVE…..

HIS REASON WAS YOU….

"In everything give thanks: for this is the will of God in Christ Jesus concerning you."

1theo5:18

"Then they took away the stone from the place where the dead was laid. And Jesus lifted up his eyes, and said, Father, I thank thee that thou hast heard me."

John 11:41

"And Jesus took the loaves; and when he had given thanks, he distributed to the disciples, and the disciples to them that were set down; and likewise of the fishes as much as they would."

John 6:11

Prayer point for protection

It is written; *"do not be afraid of sudden terror; nor of the trouble from the wicked when it comes; for the Lord will be your confidence. And will keep your foot from being caught."* **(Proverb 3:26).**

Therefore, O Lord, cover us and our loved ones from the activities of terrorists, in Jesus name!

It is written; *"avenge me of my adversary."* **(Luke. 18:3).**

Therefore, O Lord, arise and avenge us of all my adversaries in the name of Jesus!

It is written; *"they fought from the heavens; the stars from their courses fought against Sisera."* **(Judges. 5:20).**

Therefore O heavens, fight for us in Jesus name!

It is written; *"I will purge the rebels from among you, and those who transgress against Me; I will bring them out of the country where they dwell, but they shall not enter the land of Israel. They will know that I am the Lord."* **(Ezekiel. 20:38)**

Therefore, O Lord, purge and sanitize our household in the name of Jesus!

It is written; *"Then it was so, after all your wickedness – "woe, woe to you!" says the Lord God"* **(Ezekiel. 16:23)**

Therefore, woe unto all the vessels that the enemy is using to do us harm in the name of Jesus!

It is written; *"Behold therefore, I stretch out My hand against you, admonished your allotment, and gave you up to the will of those who hate you..."* **(Ezek. 16:27)**

Therefore, let our enemies be delivered into the hands of their enemies in Jesus name!

It is written; *"You shall be for fuel of fire; your blood shall be in the midst of the land. You shall not be remembered, for I the Lord have spoken."* **(Ezekiel. 21:32)**

Therefore, let all our spiritual enemies become fuel for divine fire in Jesus name!

It is written; *"Then they will know that I am the Lord, when I have set a fire in Egypt and all her helpers are destroyed."* **(Ezekiel. 30:8).**

Therefore, O Lord, let all the helpers of our enemies be destroyed in the name of Jesus.

It is written; *"And the people to whom they prophesy shall be cast out in the streets of Jerusalem because of the famine and the sword; they will have no one to bury them – them nor their wives, their sons nor their daughters – for I will pour their wickedness on them."* **(Jer. 14:16).**

Therefore, O Lord, pour the wickedness of those who seek to destroy us upon their own heads in the name of Jesus!

It is written; *"Call together the archers against Babylon. All you who bend the bow encamp against it all around; let none of them escape. Repay her according to her work; According to all she has done, do to her; for she has been poured against the Lord, against the Holy one of Israel."* **(Jer. 50:29).**

Therefore, let all the hosts of the Lord turn against our spiritual enemies in Jesus name!

It is written; *"Let God arise, let His enemies be scattered; let those also who hate him flee before him."* **(Psalms. 68:1).**

Therefore, O God, arise and let all your enemies in our lives be scattered in Jesus name!

Therefore, O Lord, pour the wickedness of those who seek to destroy us upon their own heads in the name of Jesus!

It is written; *"And He that searches the hearts knows what the mind of the spirit is, because He makes intercession for the saints according to the will of God."* **(Romans 8:27)**

Therefore, the intercessory prayers of Jesus, who is seated on the right hand of the throne of God, will not be in vain over our lives, in the name of Jesus.

It is written; *"The Lord is your keeper; the Lord is the shade at your right hand. The sun shall not strike you by day, nor the moon by night. The Lord shall preserve you from all evil; He shall preserve your soul. The Lord shall preserve your going out and your coming in from this time forth, and even forevermore."* **(Psalms. 121:5-8)**

Therefore, O Lord, spread your covering of fire and the blood of Jesus over us and our loved ones, in the name of Jesus.

It is written; *"Rejoice always, pray without ceasing, in everything give thanks; for this is the will of God in Christ Jesus for you."* **(1 Thess. 5:16:18).**

Therefore, we thank you Father, for raising a spiritual shield over our loved ones and us. Thank you for giving us the heart for appreciating everything you are doing for us. Thank you for filling our hearts and our home with joy and peace that surpasses all understanding. Blessed be your name for all the answers to our prayers in the name of Jesus!

You are holy, holy, Lord God Almighty, who was and is and is to come, Amen!

O Lord, let our season of divine intervention appear in the name of Jesus!

O you gates in the heavenlies standing against our destiny, lift up your heads in the name of Jesus!

O you gates in the waters standing against our destiny, lift up your heads in the name of Jesus!

O you gates in the earth standing against our destiny, lift up your heads in the name of Jesus!

O you gates under the earth standing against our destiny, lift up your heads in the name of Jesus!

O God, arise and destroy every gate keeper assigned against our lives in the name of Jesus!

We break the backbone of every spirit of scarcity in our lives in the name of Jesus!

O Lord anoint our eyes to see divine opportunities in the name of Jesus!

Lord let every blindness to the treasures of our lives be cleared in the name of Jesus!

Let our divine helpers appear in the name of Jesus!

We declare, O Lord, that the rest of our lives will be better than the first part, in Jesus name!

We declare, O Lord that will overcome obstacles and defeat every enemy, in Jesus name!

We declare, O Lord that every blessing and promise that you put in our hearts will come to pass because this is our time for favour, in Jesus name!

We declare, O Lord that this is a new season of increase in our lives. We speak health, wisdom, creativity, divine connections and supernatural opportunities. They are coming our way, in Jesus name!

We declare, O Lord that we choose faith over fear. We are victorious in faith, in Jesus name!

We declare, O Lord that that we are not just surviving, this is our time to thrive in prosperity, in Jesus name!

We declare, O Lord that we will believe that we have received in the spirit even though we do not see anything happening in the flesh, in Jesus name!

We declare, O Lord that our rewards are being transferred to us because we remain in faith, in Jesus name!

We declare, O Lord that doubt will not ruin our optimistic spirit, in Jesus name!

We declare, O Lord that we are prisoners of hope and get up every morning expecting your favour, in Jesus name!

We declare, O Lord that you will do amazing things in our lives, in Jesus name!

We declare, O Lord that we are closer to your abundant blessing than we think, our time has come, your promises will come to pass, in Jesus name!

We declare, O Lord that we will stay in an attitude of faith and expectation, in Jesus name!

We declare, O Lord that we are not worried, we know that you are our vindicator. It may seem to be taking a long time, but we will reap in due season if trust in you Lord, in Jesus name!

We declare, O Lord that you know the secret petitions our heart and we believe that they will come to fulfilment, in Jesus name!

We declare, O Lord that you will open new doors for us, in Jesus name!

We declare, O Lord that we will see your goodness, in Jesus name!

We declare, O Lord that this is our time to believe because favour is coming our way, in Jesus name!

We declare, O Lord that you have paved the way to abundant prosperity for us, prosperity more than we can every dream of or imagine, for your sake, in Jesus name!

We declare, O Lord that in your eyes our future is extremely bright, in Jesus name!

We declare, O Lord that we will rise higher and higher and see more of your favour and blessings and we will live the prosperous life you have in store for us, in Jesus name!

We declare, O Lord that we may have a lot of turmoil, but we know that everything is going to be alright, in Jesus name!

We declare, O Lord that we have faith because we have put you first, in Jesus name!

We thank you, O Lord that our set time for favour is here, in Jesus name!

We declare, O Lord that our hour of deliverance has come, in Jesus name!

We declare, O Lord that there is no limit to what we can do, in Jesus name!

We declare, O Lord that there is no obstacle we cannot overcome, in Jesus name!

We declare, O Lord that that we have seen your accomplishments and they are good, in Jesus name!

We declare, O Lord that there is no challenge that is too great for us because you are with us, in Jesus name!

We declare, O Lord that you always succeed, in Jesus name!

We declare, O Lord that there is no financial difficulty or situation in our lives that is too great for you to resolve, in Jesus name!

We declare, O Lord that you are our Father Jehovah Jireh and that you own everything and you are our provider, in Jesus name!

We declare, O Lord that your promises declare that we are destined to live a victorious life, in Jesus name!

We declare, O Lord that we are your children, in Jesus name!

We declare, O Lord that the seeds of increase, success and promotion are taking a new root; your favour will spring forth in our lives in a great way; we will see new seasons of blessings and new seasons of your favour. It's our time to have abundant faith, in Jesus name!

O Lord, it is written; according to your faith, it will be done unto you. Ps. 2:8 says "ask me and I will give you the nations as your inheritance."

Therefore, we ask you Lord to fulfil our highest hopes and dreams, in Jesus name!

We ask you this day, O Lord to give us our abundant blessing now, in Jesus name!

We dare to exercise our faith by asking you O Lord so that we may receive indeed, in Jesus name!

We thank you O Lord that for encouraging our faith, in Jesus name!

We declare, O Lord that this is our time for favour, in Jesus name!

We declare, O Lord that this is our time to prosper abundantly, in Jesus name!

We declare, O Lord that this is our time to have instant answers to prayer, in Jesus name!

We declare, O Lord that this is our time to ask and receive, in Jesus name!

We declare, O Lord that this is our time to thank you and testify for answered prayer, in Jesus name!

We declare, O Lord that we are blessed and that goodness and mercy are following us right now, in Jesus name!

We declare, O Lord that you favour is surrounding us like a shield – you prosper us even in the desert, in Jesus name!

We declare, O Lord that you have great things for us in the spirit and that you have already released favour into our prayers, in Jesus name!

We declare, O Lord that you are a great and Holy God, in Jesus name!

It is written; *"Delight yourself in the Lord and he will give you the desires of your heart."* **(Ps 37:4).**

We therefore declare, O Lord that we delight in you because you are our Father God and because we are your children you have made us the head and not the tail. You want to take us to a new level of prosperity, in Jesus name!

We declare, O Lord that because we are your children, we are more than conquerors, in Jesus name!

We declare, O Lord that we are blessed and you supply all our needs. We have more than enough, in Jesus name!

We declare, O Lord that we have abundant favour indeed, in Jesus name!

We declare, O Lord that we are filled indeed with the presence of the Holy Spirit, in Jesus name!

We declare, O Lord that we have abundant faith indeed, in Jesus name!

We declare, O Lord that you have answered our prayers, in Jesus name!

We declare, O Lord that our debts are all paid up, in Jesus name!

We declare, O Lord that we are healthy, in Jesus name!

We declare, O Lord that we have no lack and that we have more than enough, in Jesus name!

We declare, O Lord that we are extremely blessed so much that we can bless your kingdom, in Jesus name!

We declare, O Lord that we are extremely blessed so much that we can bless others, in Jesus name!

We declare, O Lord that we have entered into an anointing of ease, in Jesus name!

We declare, O Lord that for every opportunity we have missed, every chance we've blown, you will turn the clock and bring bigger and better things across our path , in Jesus name!

We declare, O Lord that we will not settle for less than your best, in Jesus name!

Please restore the time that we have lost, O Lord that, in Jesus name!

Restore our victories, O Lord, in Jesus name!

Restore our lost joy, lost peace, lost health, lost insight, lost faith, lost dedication and desire to please you, we declare, O Lord in Jesus name!

We declare, O Lord that you use what was meant for our harm to our advantage, in Jesus name!

We declare, O Lord that you are a faithful God, in Jesus name!

We declare, O Lord that you will blossom our lives in ways that we can never imagine, in Jesus name!

We know, O Lord that you will bless us abundantly, in Jesus name!

We know, O Lord that you will provide divine connections, in Jesus name!

We declare, O Lord that we are not suffering – we are blessed, in Jesus name!

We declare, O Lord that our difficulties will give way to new growth, new opportunities, and new vision, in Jesus name!

O Lord let us see your blessing bloom in our lives in ways we would never dreamt possible, in Jesus name!

We declare, O Lord that we will stay in faith, so that what was meant to stop us will not be a stumbling block but a stepping stone taking us to a higher level, in Jesus name!

We declare, O Lord that we are not ordinary, but we are children of the most high God, in Jesus name!

We declare, O Lord that we created to rise above problems, in Jesus name!

We declare victory over strife O Lord, in Jesus name!

We declare, O Lord that no weapon formed against us shall prosper, in Jesus name!

We declare, O Lord that we are healthy and that no sickness shall live in us, in Jesus name!

We declare, O Lord that triumph is our birthright, in Jesus name!

We declare, O Lord that our setbacks are simply setups for greater comebacks that will place us to be better than we were before, in Jesus name!

We declare, O Lord that with you all things are possible, in Jesus name!

We declare, O Lord that we are in agreement with you. We know you have supernatural favour in store for us. You have supernatural opportunities, supernatural healing and supernatural restoration, in Jesus name!

We declare, O Lord that you want to do unusual things in our lives, in Jesus name!

We declare, O Lord that in faith, we have expectation deep in our spirits, in Jesus name!

We declare, O Lord that this will not be a survival year but a supernatural year in which you will abundantly come through for us, in Jesus name!

We believe, O Lord that you have come through for us, in Jesus name!

We declare, O Lord that because we hope in you, we will not be put to shame, in Jesus name!

We declare, O Lord that your word is right and true, you are faithful in all you do, in Jesus name!

We declare, O Lord that you are our refuge and strength, an ever present helper, in Jesus name!

We declare, O Lord that we will cast our cares on you and you will sustain us, you will never let the righteous fall, in Jesus name!

We declare, O Lord that you are the strength of our hearts and our portion forever, in Jesus name!

We declare, O Lord that you are our dwelling, therefore, no harm will befall us and no disaster will come near our tent, in Jesus name!

We declare, O Lord that you are our refuge and our fortress, in Jesus name!

We declare, O Lord that you will command your angels concerning us to guard us in all our ways, in Jesus name!

We declare, O Lord that even in darkness the light will dawn for us, in Jesus name!

We declare, O Lord that your word is eternal and stands firm in the heavens, in Jesus name!

We declare, O Lord that your faithfulness will continue throughout all generations, in Jesus name!

We declare, O Lord that you will keep us from harm; you will watch over our lives; you will watch over our coming and our going both now and for evermore, in Jesus name! **(Ps. 121)**

Thank you O Lord for the assurance that you are watching over us even when we sleep, in Jesus name! **(Ps. 13:5-6)**

We declare, O Lord that you will drive those that do evil away from us and that you will protect us from their influence, in Jesus name! **(Ps. 66:1-4)**

We will shout with joy to you O Lord, we will sing the glory of your name and make your praise glorious. How awesome are your deeds! So great is your power that your enemies cringe before you, in Jesus name!

We declare, O Lord that that we will give you thanks for you answered us, in Jesus name! **(Ps. 118:21)**

We declare, O Lord that we will praise you with all our hearts; before the gods we will sing your praise. We will bow down towards your Holy temple and will praise your name for your love and your faithfulness, for you have exalted above all things, your name and your word, in Jesus name! **(Ps. 138:1-3)**

Amen!

Why do most people complain in life?

It is written *"And when the people complained, it displeased the Lord: and the Lord heard it; and his anger was kindled; and the fire of the Lord burnt among them, and consumed them that were in the uttermost parts of the camp."* **Number11:1**

Most of us complain and get stressed out in life because we lack the spirit of thanksgiving in our heart. Thanksgiving is a spirit of gratitude. It makes us grateful and appreciative in life. Thanksgiving have power to multiply our blessings in life.

Every time we give thanks well, we set our self-up for the next miracle in our life. You see! Thanksgiving have power to setup the next miracle and also power to preserve our blessing. Unless you embrace the attitude of thanksgiving, you will forever complain and get depressed in life.

I encourage you to look around your life and find one reason to thank God. He kept you alive. David said I laid me down and slept; I awaked; for the Lord sustained me.

Most people complain because they do not believe God.

God will never change His deity because of our unbelief. Before you were born his is God, after you will die He will still remain God. So many of us do not give thanks well to God because we do not be in Him.

It is written *"Because they regard not the works of the Lord, nor the operation of his hands, he shall destroy them, and not build them up."* **Psalms28:5**

It is written *"Jesus said unto him, If thou canst believe, all things are possible to him that believeth."* **(Mark9:23).**

You must develop the mindset of thanksgiving. Honestly speaking, that's the only way to diligently reward our life.

It is written *"... for he that cometh to God must believe that he is, and that he is a rewarder of them that diligently seek him."* **(Hebrews11:6).**

For unless we embrace thanksgiving as a lifestyle to God, unbelief will always hinder our blessing from God. If we don't connect to God through praise, and worship, meditation, and in prayers, we should definitely connect to God through thanksgiving.

CHAPTER 1
What is thanksgiving?

"In everything give thanks: for this is the will of God in Christ Jesus concerning you." **1theo5:18**

Thanksgiving is an attitude of gratitude. By this I mean appreciating God in anticipation of what He will do in our lives. Thanksgiving means appreciating God for life, for our love ones, and families, our friends, and colleagues.

Thanksgiving is the will of God. Every time you give thanks, you are doing the will of the Father. We are told, *"In everything give thanks: for this is the will of God in Christ Jesus concerning you."*

Whenever thanksgiving become a way of life, signs, and wonders becomes our natural experience. The story of the ten lepers is a fascinating account of quality thanks to God. Ten lepers were cleansed, but only one returned to Jesus to say thank you very much. And this fellow that returned to say thank you was made perfectly whole.

It is written *"And one of them, when he saw that he was healed, turned back, and with a loud voice glorified God, And fell down on his face at his feet, giving him thanks: and he was a Samaritan. And Jesus answering said, Were there not ten cleansed? but where are the nine?"* **Luke17:15-17**

Thanksgiving simply means appreciating the acts of God upon our lives. We were told by the Holy Scriptures, *"Because they regard not the works of the Lord, nor the operation of his hands, he shall destroy them, and not build them up."* **Psalms28:5**

If we must experience breakthrough in life we must embrace thanksgiving as a lifestyle. Every time you thank God well, God send a new blessing into your life.

Jesus –the master, took advantage of this mystery during his earthly ministry. At one point during Jesus's ministry Jesus asked Philip a strange question, I should say. When Jesus then lifted up his eyes, and saw a great company come unto him, he saith unto Philip, Whence shall we buy bread, that these may eat?

Chapter 1 - What is Thanksgiving?

The bible recorded that he only said this to surprise Philip, simply because he knew what to do. It is written And this he said to prove him: for he himself knew what he would do.

What did he do?

"And Jesus took the loaves; and when he had given thanks, he distributed to the disciples, and the disciples to them that were set down; and likewise of the fishes as much as they would." **John6:11**

Every time you give God praise by thanking Him, the earth yields her increase. It is written *"Let the people praise thee, O God; let all the people praise thee. Then shall the earth yield her increase; and God, even our own God, shall bless us."* **Psalms67:5-6.**

Thanksgiving is an affirmation of our faith in Christ Jesus. One of the primary ways for you to be certified as a Holy Spirit filled believer is the spirit of thanksgiving. The Lord Jesus looks into our heart, and not upon our appearance, or faces.

It is written *"But the Lord said unto Samuel, Look not on his countenance, or on the height of his stature; because I have refused him: for the Lord seeth not as man seeth; for man looketh on the outward appearance, but the Lord looketh on the heart."* **1samuel16:7**

God is spirit. This Holy Spirit look for motives and intention in life. A lot of people will do nothing for you, unless you do something for them. Well that is not God. In the kingdom of God, we thank God in anticipation for something to be done upon our lives.

It is written *"And if ye have not been faithful in that which is another man's, who shall give you that which is your own?"*

Often people are not faithful in handling anything that does not belong to them. They do not care much about it, as long as it does not belong to them. Some of us are mere men pleasers. We only want to be heard and seen by other. I call it eye service. God look for our intentions and the motive of the our heart.

Chapter 1 - What is Thanksgiving?

It is written *"Not with eyeservice, as menpleasers; but as the servants of Christ, doing the will of God from the heart."* **Ephesians 6:6**

How can you be cheating, lying in your life, always planning evil against your brother, yet you come to give God thanks. The say to you in particular

"Therefore if thou bring thy gift to the altar, and there rememberest that thy brother hath ought against thee; Leave there thy gift before the altar, and go thy way; first be reconciled to thy brother, and then come and offer thy gift." **Mathew 5:23-24**

Some of us only talk the talk we do not walk the talk. If I am permitted to speak in that manner. With the words of our mouth, we honor God, but the truth is that, our heart is too far away from him.

"Wherefore the Lord said, Forasmuch as this people draw near me with their mouth, and with their lips do honour me, but have removed their heart far from me, and their fear toward me is taught by the precept of men:" **Isaiah 29:13**

Often God will test our heart like He did to this king, in this scripture below, *"Howbeit in the business of the ambassadors of the princes of Babylon, who sent unto him to enquire of the wonder that was done in the land, God left him, to try him that he might know all that was in his heart."* **2chronicle32:31.**

Genuine thanks to God must come from our heart. For God ponder our heart. Every way of a man is right in his own eyes: but the Lord pondereth the hearts. **Proverb21:2**

God searches our heart. *"And ye shall seek me, and find me, when ye shall search for me with all your heart."* **Jer29:13**

We cannot fake thanksgiving. It is either you are genuinely thanking God for his goodness upon your life. Or you are barely having a mere celebration. Just like I say all the time, praise speaks of how great and powerful God is, worship speaks of His Holiness, but thanks giving explains how good God has been to our lives. I encourage you to look for any one reason and say "THANK YOU GOD."

Chapter 1 - What is Thanksgiving?

Every time you are depressed, you are living in the past, whenever you are anxious you are living in the future. But when you are at peace. You are living in the present. May you live in the present in the mighty Name of Jesus.

I encourage everyone to make it a lifestyle to thank God daily for His benefits. The psalmist said "Blessed be the Lord, who daily loadeth us with benefits, even the God of our salvation. Selah."

"O give thanks unto the Lord; for he is good: for his mercy endureth for ever." **Psalms136:1**

"O give thanks unto the God of gods: for his mercy endureth for ever." **Psalms136:2**

"O give thanks to the Lord of lords: for his mercy endureth for ever." **Psalms136:3**

"O give thanks unto the Lord, for he is good: for his mercy endureth for ever." **Psalms107:1**

"Let the redeemed of the Lord say so, whom he hath redeemed from the hand of the enemy;" **Psalms 107:2**

"It is a good thing to give thanks unto the Lord, and to sing praises unto thy name, O Most High." **Psalms 92:1**

"To shew forth thy lovingkindness in the morning, and thy faithfulness every night." **Psalms 92:2**

These scriptures above are helpful links to offer a prayer of thanks giving unto God daily.

CHAPTER 2
How do I give Quality Thanks to God.

"Enter into his gates with thanksgiving, and into his courts with praise: be thankful unto him, and bless his name." **Psalms100:4**

Although without quality thanks no one can enter His gate, nor His court. Quality thanks must come from the heart. By this I mean, it must come from our spirit man. The above scripture says Enter into his gates with thanksgiving, and into his courts with praise: be thankful unto him, and bless his name. You and I have no chance to enter His gate without thanksgiving.

The Psalmist said *"Those that be planted in the house of the Lord shall flourish in the courts of our God."* It my own understanding only genuine thanks giver will flourish in His court.

As long as you are bitter, jealous, envious, contentious, you will never get a chance at His gate. Recall with me… in thy presence is fulness of joy; at thy right hand there are pleasures for evermore. The truth is being thankful isn't just for the Thanksgiving holiday alone. It must become a daily ritual for every genuine believer.

The Holy bible tells us to be *"thankful in everything, that means in all circumstances"* **1 Thessalonians 5:18.**

Whenever we are overwhelmed with challenges, and worried about tomorrow, there is only one way out. Give God thanks for what He has done thus far in your life.

We must reflect on all that God has done for us in time past, and be thankful for everything. We must always to pray, praise and thank God for life. I like to say life is a gift, it is not a privilege. You are not supposed to be alive, but you are here by the grace of God. We thank God.

Chapter 2 - How to give Quality Thanks to God

Although the holiday-thanksgiving is a wonderful time to celebrate with family and friends. It must become a daily ritual for us as believers. By this I mean a way of life.

Have you ever spent time in prayers thanking God?

It is written *"Be careful for nothing; but in everything by prayer and supplication with thanksgiving let your requests be made known unto God."* **Phil4:6**

Paul and Silas took advantage of giving thanks in their prayers. It is written *"And at midnight Paul and Silas prayed, and sang praises unto God: and the prisoners heard them."* **Acts16:25**

Our faith and trust automatically will grow if we develop a lifestyle of giving thanks to God daily.

Prayer 1: A Daily Thanksgiving Prayer

Prayer 1: A Daily Thanksgiving Prayer

"Dear God, Thank you for your awesome power and work in our lives, thank you for your greatness and for your blessings over us. Thank you for your great love and care. Thank you for your sacrifice so that we might have freedom and life. Forgive us for when we don't thank you enough. Amen"

Prayer 2: A Prayer for a Thankful Heart

"Lord Jesus, Instruct me to offer you a heart of thanksgiving and praise in all my daily experiences of life. Teach me to be joyful always, to pray continually, and to give thanks in all my circumstances. I accept them as your will for my life. Amen"

Prayer 3: A Prayer of Thanks

"Father I thank you for my life, family, and love ones, oftentimes life challenges pull me down and I find difficult to give you thanks. Open my heart to recognize all the good things you have done so far in my life. I thank you Jesus for my life. Amen."

Chapter 2 - How to give Quality Thanks to God

Prayer 4: A Prayer to Teach children to be Thankfulness

"Lord Jesus, I pray that you will put it in the heart of every child to be thankful in life. Father give them a purpose and let your joy become their strength. I thank you for all you have done in our lives. Amen"

Prayer 5: A Thanksgiving Day Prayer

"Our Heavenly Father:
We thank Thee for food and remember the hungry.
We thank Thee for health and remember the sick.
We thank Thee for friends and remember the friendless.
We thank Thee for freedom and remember the enslaved.
May these remembrances stir us to service. That Thy gifts to us may be used for others. Amen."

Prayer 7: 17 Confession of Gratitude

"Thank you, God for the times You have said "no." They have helped me depend on You so much more.

Thank you, God, for unanswered prayer. It reminds me that You know what's best for me, even when my opinion differs from Yours.

Thank You, Lord, for the things you have withheld from me. You have protected me from what I may never realize.

Thank You Jesus, for the doors You have closed in my life. And for the present open door in my life. Lord let your will be done in my life. Amen

Thank you, Jesus for food on my table daily.
Thank you, Lord, for the alone times in my life. Those times have forced me to lean in closer to You.

Thank you, God, for the uncertainties I've experienced. They have deepened my trust in You.

Chapter 2 - How to give Quality Thanks to God

Thank You, Lord, for the times You came through for me when I didn't even know I needed a rescue.

Thank You, Lord, for the losses I have experienced. They have been a reminder that You are my greatest gain.

Thank You, God, for the tears I have shed. They have kept my heart soft and mold-able.
Thank You, God, for the times I haven't been able to control my circumstances. They have reminded me that You are sovereign and on the throne.

Thank You, God, for the life of every living person you planted somehow into my life. I give you praise for what you have done and for what you are doing in my life.

Thank You, God that I have an inheritance in the heavenly places...I desire to be with you one day in eternity. Amen"

Thank You, God, for the greatest gift You could ever give me: forgiveness through Your perfect Son's death on the cross on my behalf.

The Power of Thanksgiving by Franklin N. Abazie

Thank You, God, for the righteousness You credited toward me, through the death and resurrection of Jesus. It's a righteousness I could never earn or attain on my own.

Thank You, Father, that You know me, You hear me, and You see my tears. Remind me through difficult times that You are my God, You are on the throne, and You are eternally good.

And thank You, Lord, not only for my eternal salvation, but for the salvation You afford every day of my life as You save me from myself, my foolishness, my own limited insights, and my frailties in light of Your power and strength."

Chapter 2 - How to give Quality Thanks to God

CONCLUSION

"It is a good thing to give thanks unto the Lord, and to sing praises unto thy name, O Most High." **Psalms 92:1**

If we have not been giving thanks even in our prayers, then we have not been living right. Thanksgiving must become a daily ritual for every believer.

"Therefore if any man be in Christ, he is a new creature: old things are passed away; behold, all things are become new." **2cor 5:17**

Now repeat this Prayer after me;

Say Lord Jesus, I accept you today, as my Lord and my savior, forgive me of my sins wash me with your blood. Right now, I believe, I am sanctified, I am save, I am free, I am free from the Power of sin to serve the Lord Jesus. Thank you Lord for saving me. Amen.

Congratulations: YOU ARE NOW A BORN AGAIN CHRISTIAN

What must I do to determine my divine visitation?

To determine divine visitation you must be born again. The word says as many as received him, to them gave He power to become the sons of God. Even to them that believe on his name.

To qualify for divine visitation do the following sincerely;

1) Acknowledge that you are a sinner and that He died for you. **Rom3:23**.

2) Repent of your sins. **Acts 3:19, Luke13:5, 2Peter3:9**

3) Believe in your heart that Jesus died for your sin. **Romans10:10**

4) Confess Jesus as the Lord over your life. **Romans10:10, Acts2:21**

Chapter 2 - How to give Quality Thanks to God

Now repeat this Prayer after me

Say Lord Jesus, I accept you today, as my Lord and my savior, forgive me of my sins wash me with your blood. Right now, I believe, I am sanctified, I am save, I am free, I am free from the Power of sin to serve the Lord Jesus. Thank you Lord for saving me. Amen.

Congratulations: YOU ARE NOW A BORN AGAIN CHRISTAIN

I adjure you to watch the Spirit of God bear witness with your Spirit confirming His word with signs following. The word says The Spirit itself beareth witness with our spirit, that we are the children of God. Join a bible believing church or join us on our weekly and Sunday worship services at 343 Sanford Avenue Newark New Jersey 07106.

WISDOM KEYS

Every Productive Society is a society heading to the top

Millions of Nigerians run away from Nigeria, very few Nigerians stay in Nigeria.

My decision to return Nigeria is the will of God for my life

My short coming in America after 18 years, trained me to be wise, to think, reflect and reason appropriately.

If you train your mind to reason it will train your hands to earn money.

It is absurd to use the money of the heathen to build the kingdom of the living God.

Every Ministry reveals its agenda and goal either at the beginning or at the end. Be careful of your life it is your first Ministry.

The average American mind is conditioned for a continual quest to get new things and (discard the former) and throw away old things.

Chapter 2 - How to give Quality Thanks to God

When I considered well, my BMW jeep became my initial deposit for the work of the ministry in Nigeria

Everyone is waiting for you to change your mind until you change your thinking nothing changes around you.

Multiple academic degrees in other discipline gave me the chance to think, reflect and reason

What so everyone are thinking and reflecting at the moment reveals you to the time and the now factor

All events and intents are the product of precise thought processes, accurate reason every event is designed for a designated timeline

Wisdom is your ability to think, to create and invent. If you can think wise enough you will come out of penury

The distance between you and success is your creative ability to think reason and reflect accurate.

Success is the result of hard work, commitment resolve and determination learning from past mistakes and failing.

If you organize your mind you have organized your life and destiny.

There is a thin line between success and failure. If you look above and beyond you are on your way to success.

Wealth is your ability to think, power is your ability to reason and success is your ability to be informed.

If you can make use of your mind by thinking and reasoning God will make use of your life and destiny.

Think and Be Great

Reflect, Reason, think and be great

Famous people are born of woman

Chapter 2 - How to give Quality Thanks to God

That you will make it is your intention; that you will survive is your resolve, that you will succeed with changes is your determination, personal efforts and hard work.

No man was born a failure. Lack of vision is the end product of failure.

Working with mental patients encourages and aspire me to be a productive observant and dedicated to my assignment.

Successful people are not magicians, it is the will power combined with hard work, and determination and a resolve to succeed that make them succeed.

In the unequivocal state of the mind, intention is not a location or a position it is the state of the mind.

So many people think that they think. The mind is used to think reflect and reason. You will remain blind with your eye open until you can see with your mind by thinking.

There is no favoritism in accurate and precise calculation

Although knowledge is power, information is the key and gateway to a great future.

It will take the hand of God to move the hand of man.

With the backing of the great wise God, nothing will disconnect you from your inheritance.

As long as you have wisdom and understanding of God, Satan and evil cannot manipulate your life and destiny.

You have come this far by yourself judgment and decision you have made in the past, now lean and listen to God for another dimension of greatness.

Great people are common people it is extra ordinary effort and the price of sacrifice that produces greatness.

As a mental direct care worker I saw a great pastor and a motivational speaker within myself.

Menial job does not reduce your self-worth, until you resolve to achieve greatness see greatness in all you do; you will never count in your community

Chapter 2 - How to give Quality Thanks to God

The principle of Jesus will solve your gambling and addiction problems

The man of Jesus will lead you into heaven,

Everyone have their self-appraisal and what they think about you. Until you discover yourself other opinion about you will alter the real you.

Supervisors and directors are just a position in the chain of command in a work place. Never allow your supervisor hierarchy to alter your opinion about yourself.

Everyone can come out of debt if they make up their mind.

That I am not a decision maker at work does not diminish my contribution to my world.

Although it appears like it was a poor decision to accept a direct care employment at a psychiatric hospital as I reflect of my nine years of experience, it became apparent that I have learnt and experienced enough for my next assignment.

Self-encouragement and determination is a resolve of the heart.

The Power of Thanksgiving by Franklin N. Abazie

If you are determined to make a difference, and do the things that make a difference you will eventually make a difference.

Good things do not come easy

Short cuts will cut your life short.

Those who look ahead move ahead.

Life is all about making an impact. In your life time strive to make an impact in your community.

Make friends and connect with people who are moving ahead of you in life.

If you can look around well you have come a long way in your life, made a lot of difference and realized a lot of success in life.

If you are my old friend, hurry up to reach out to me before I become a stranger to you.

Everything I am blessed with inspirations from God, that change my definition and interpretation of the world around me.

I thought I was stagnant and lonely until I looked around and noticed my children running around and my wife cooking.

Chapter 2 - How to give Quality Thanks to God

At 40 I resigned my Job to seek the Lord forever.

My ministry took a drastic rise to the top when the wisdom of God visited me with knowledge and understanding.

You will be a better person if you understand the characteristics of your personality – your mood swings attitudes and habits.

It is the seed of love you sow into the heart of a child and a woman that you reap in due time.

Love is not selfish, love share everything including the concealed secrets of the mind.

As long as you have a prayer life and a bible; you will never feel lonely, rejected and idle in the race of life.

When good friends disconnect from you, let them go, they might have seen something new in a different direction.

Confidence in yourself and in God is the only way to bring you out of captivity

Never train a child to waste his/her time.

The mind is the greatest assets of a great future.

You walk by common sense run by principles and fly by instruction.

Those who fly in flight of life fly alone.

Up in the air you are alone. No one can toll you accept the compass of knowledge and information

I have seen a tolling vehicle I have seen a tolling ship I have never seen a tolling airplane.

I exercise my judgment and make a decision every minute of the day.

Decisions are crucial, critical and vital with reference to your future.

So many people wish for a great future. You can only work towards a great future.

Your celebrity status began when you discovered your talent. What are you good at? Work at it with all commitment.

Prayers will sustain you but the wisdom of God will prosper you.

When I met Oyedepo, his teachings changed my perspective, but when I met Ibiyeomie; His teaching changed my perception.

Chapter 2 - How to give Quality Thanks to God

I will be successful in ministry if only I concentrate and focus my energy in the work of the ministry.

It took the late Dr. Vincent Pearle Norman's book to open my mind towards kingdom success.

CHAPTER 3

PRAYER OF SALVATION

"Neither is there salvation in any other: for there is none other name under heaven given among men, whereby we must be saved." **Acts4:12.**

There is only one name that will take us all into heaven.

What must I do to determine my salvation?

To be saved we must be born again! The word says as many as received him, to them gave He power to become the sons of God. Even to them that believe on his name.

To qualify for divine visitation do the following sincerely,

1) Acknowledge that you are a sinner and that He died for you. **Rom3:23.**

2) Repent of your sins. **Acts 3:19, Luke13:5, 2Peter3:9**

Chapter 3 - Prayer of Salvation

3) Believe in your heart that Jesus died for your sin. **Romans10:10**

4) Confess Jesus as the Lord over your life. **Romans10:10, Acts2:21**

Now repeat this Prayer after me

Say Lord Jesus, I accept you today, as my Lord and my savior, forgive me of my sins wash me with your blood. Right now, I believe, I am sanctified, I am save, I am free, I am free from the Power of sin to serve the Lord Jesus. Thank you Lord for saving me. Amen.

Congratulations:

YOU ARE NOW A BORN AGAIN CHRISTAIN

AGAIN I SAY TO YOU CONGRATULATION

I adjure you to watch the Spirit of God bear witness with your Spirit confirming His word with signs following. The word says The Spirit itself beareth witness with our spirit, that we are the children of God.

MIRACLE CARE OUTREACH

"...But that the members should have the same care one for another" **1cor12:25**

We are all members of the body of Christ. Jesus commanded us to love our neighbor as ourselves. This includes caring for one another as a member of one body. True love is expressed in caring and giving. The word says for God so Love He gave….

Reach out to someone in need of Jesus, help someone in crisis find Christ. Look out and prove your love to Jesus by caring and inviting your friends and associates to find Jesus the Healer.

Invite your friends to our Home Care Cell Fellowship (Miracle chapel Intl Satellite fellowship) In the USA at 33 Schley Street Newark New Jersey 07112.

If you are in Nigeria—**MIRACLE OF GOD MINISTRIES**

A.K.A "MIRACLE CHAPEL INTL" Mpama –Egbu-Owerri Imo state Nigeria.

Chapter 3 - Prayer of Salvation

(Home Care Cell fellowship Group). We meet every Tuesday at 6:00pm-7:00pm.

LIFE IS NOT ALL ABOUT DURATION BUT ITS ALL ABOUT DONATION

What does the above statement mean?....

"Life consists not in accumulation of material wealth.." **Luke12:15.**

"But it's all about liberality....meaning-what you can give and share with others." **Proverb11:25.**

When you live for others--You live forever- because you out live your generation by the legacy you live behind after you depart into glory to be with the Lord. But when you live to yourself - you are reduced to self—you are easily forgotten when you die and depart in glory.

Permit me to admonish you today to live your life to be a blessing to a soul connected to you today.

I want you to know that so many souls are connected and looking up to you, and through you so many souls will be saved and rescued from destruction. Will you disciple someone today to find Jesus Christ?

"As a genuine Christian; it is your duty to evangelize Jesus Christ to all you meet on your way. Jesus is still in the healing business-Jesus is still doing miracles from time of old to now.

Therefore tell someone about Jesus Christ today, disciple and bring them to Church."

John 1:45 Philip findeth Nathanael....

Please to prove the sincerity of your love for God today; please become a soul winner. The dignity of your Christianity is hidden in your boldness to proclaim and evangelize Jesus Christ to all you meet on your way.

There is a question mark on the integrity of your Christianity until you become a life soul winner. Invite someone to join us worship the Lord Jesus this coming Sunday.

Chapter 3 - Prayer of Salvation

MIRACLE OF GOD MINISTRIES

PILLARS OF THE COMMISSION

We Believe Preach and Practice the following,

1) We believe and preach Salvation to every living human being

2) We believe and preach Repentance and forgiveness of sins

3) We believe and preach the baptism of the Holy Spirit and Spiritual gifts

4) We believe and teach the Prosperity

5) We believe and preach Divine Healing and Miracles (Signs &Wonder)

6) We believe and preach Faith

7) We believe and Proclaim the Power of God (Supernatural)

8) We believe and Proclaim Praise& Worship to God

9) We believe and preach Wisdom

10) We believe and preach Holiness (Consecration)

11) We believe and preach Vision

12) We believe and teach the Word of God

13) We believe and teach Success

14) We believe and practice Prayer

15) We believe and teach Deliverance

This 15 stones form the Pillars of Our Commission.

Become part of this church family and follow this great move of God.

MY HEART FELT PRAYER FOR YOU

It is my prayer that you testify today about the goodness of the Lord. I desire for you to have an encounter with our Lord Jesus Christ.

Chapter 3 - Prayer of Salvation

Now let me Pray for you:

Heavenly father may today be a day of new beginning for this precious love one. Lord God of heaven open a new chapter in the life of this precious love one reading this book today. May all their prayers be answered in the mighty name of Jesus. We thank you Jesus for hearing us. In Jesus mighty name. Amen.

*****Encounter with God******

Unless you are left alone you are not ready to encounter God. Jacob was left alone and he encountered God. I strongly urge you to create a quiet time with your God. A time of meditation and reflection. God is still omnipotent and all powerful. But you have to discover this by prayer and meditation in the word of God.

Jacob encountered God

"And Jacob was left alone; and there wrestled a man with him until the breaking of the day. And when he saw that he prevailed not against him, he touched the hollow of his thigh; and the hollow of Jacob's thigh was out of joint, as he wrestled with him. And he said, Let me go, for the day breaketh. And he said, I will not let thee go, except thou bless me. And he said unto him, What is thy name? And he said, Jacob. And he said, Thy name shall be called no more Jacob, but Israel: for as a prince hast thou power with God and with men, and hast prevailed." **Genesis 32:24-28.**

Apostle Paul encountered God

"And as he journeyed, he came near Damascus: and suddenly there shined round about him a light from heaven: And he fell to the earth, and heard a voice saying unto him, Saul, Saul, why persecutest thou me? And he said, Who art thou, Lord? And the Lord said, I am Jesus whom thou persecutest: it is hard for thee to kick against the pricks." **Acts 9:3-5**

CHAPTER 4
ABOUT THE AUTHOR

Rev Franklin N Abazie is the founding and Presiding Pastor of Miracle of God Ministries with headquarters in Newark, New Jersey USA and a branch church in Owerri- Imo State Nigeria. He is following the footsteps of one of his mentors, Oral Roberts (Healing Evangelist) of the blessed memory.

The Lord passed Oral Roberts healing mantle two days before he went to be with the Lord at age 91 into the hand of healing evangelist-Rev Franklin N Abazie in a vision.

In all his services the Power and Presence of God is present to heal all in his audience. He is an ordained man of God with a Healing Ministry reviving the healing and miracle ministry of Jesus Christ of Nazareth.

Pastor Franklin N Abazie, is called by God with a unique mandate:

"THE MOMENT IS DUE TO IMPACT YOUR WORLD THROUGH THE REVIVAL OF THE HEALING & MIRACLE MINISTRY OF JESUS CHRIST OF NAZARETH.

I AM SENDING YOU TO RESTORE HEALTH UNTO THEE AND I WILL HEAL THEE OF THY WOUNDS. SAID THE LORD OF HOST"

He is a gifted ardent Teacher of the word of God who operates also in the office of a Prophet, generating and attracting undeniable signs & wonders, special miracles and healings, with apostolic fireworks of the Holy Ghost.

He is the founding and presiding senior Pastor of this fast growing Healing ministry.

He has written over 86 inspirational, healing and transforming books covering almost all aspect of divine healing and life. He is happily married and blessed with children.

BOOKS BY REV FRANKLIN N ABAZIE

1) Commanding Abundance
2) The outcome of faith
3) Understanding the secret of prevailing prayers
4) Understanding the secret of the man God uses
5) Activating my due Season
6) Overcoming Divine Verdicts
7) The Outcome of Divine Wisdom
8) Understanding God's Restoration Mandate
9) Walking in the Victory and Authority of the truth
10) Gods Covenant Exemption
11) Destiny Restoration Pillars
12) Provoking Acceptable Praise
13) Understanding Divine Judgment
14) Activating Angelic Re-enforcement
15) Provoking Un-Merited Favor
16) The Benefits of the Speaking faith
17) Understanding Divine Arrangement

18) Understanding Divine Healing
19) The Mystery of Endurance
20) Obeying Divine Instructions
21) Understanding the Voice of God
22) Never give up on Hope
23) The prevailing Power of faith
24) Understanding Divine Prosperity
25) The Reward of Prayer
26) Covenant Keys to Answered Prayers
27) Activating the Forces of Vengeance
28) Put your faith to work
29) Where is your trust?
30) The Audacity of the Blood of Jesus
31) Redeeming Your Days
32) The force of Vision
33) Breaking the shackles of Family Curses
34) Wisdom for Marriage Stability
35) The winners Faith
36) The Prayer solution
37) The power of Prayer
38) Prayer strategy
39) The prayer that works
40) Walking in Forgiveness
41) The power of the grace of God

42) The power of Persistence
43) Overcoming Divine verdicts
44) The audacity of the blood of Jesus.
45) The prevailing power of the blood of Jesus
46) The benefit of the speaking faith.
47) Fearless faith
48) Redeeming Your Days.
49) The Supernatural Power of Prophecy
50) The companionship of the Holy Spirit
51) Understanding Divine Judgement
52) Understanding Divine Prosperity
53) Dominating Controlling Forces
54) The winners Faith
55) Destiny Restoration Pillars
56) Developing Spiritual Muscles
57) Inexplicable faith
58) The lifestyle of Prayer
59) Developing a positive attitude in life.
60) The mystery of Divine supply
61) Encounter with God's Power
62) Walking in love
63) Praying in the Spirit
64) How to provoke your testimony

65) Walking in the reality of the Anointing
66) The reality of new birth
67) The price of freedom
68) The Supernatural power of faith
69) The Power of Persistence
70) The intellectual components of Redemption
71) Overcoming Fear
72) The Force of Vision
73) Overcoming Prevailing Challenges
74) The Power of the Grace of God
75) My life & Ministry
76) The Mystery of Praise

MIRACLE OF GOD MINISTRIES

NIGERIA CRUSADE 2012

MIRACLE OF GOD MINISTRIES
NIGERIA CRUSADE 2012

MIRACLE OF GOD MINISTRIES

NIGERIA CRUSADE

2012

MIRACLE OF GOD MINISTRIES

NIGERIA CRUSADE

2012

www.ingramcontent.com/pod-product-compliance
Lightning Source LLC
Chambersburg PA
CBHW021447080526
44588CB00009B/727